The Thought
BOOK

Hardback ISBN: 978-0-9934350-0-3
.ePub ISBN: 978-0-9934350-3-4
.Mobi ISBN: 978-0-9934350-2-7

First Edition

Published by Written Mirror

www.writtenmirror.com

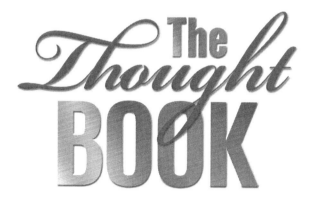

Jay Mullings

Andrew
You may be gone but you're never forgotten. Thanks for watching over me during the good and bad times.

Sylvia & Aubrey Allen
To ask for better grandparents would be a sin. I thank you for putting up with a very precocious grandchild.

This book is for you...

Jaleila
You're too young to remember, but you changed the way I look at life. You made me better than I could've ever been without you. I love you dearly.

Sisters
1-3 You already know what it is...

CB, DB, FT, IS, LG, LR, ME, ML, OW, RL, SG, SH, SV
You have all contributed to my equilibrium over the years. I truly appreciate your kindness and encouragement.

Foreword
by Dr. Ian Smith

Jay Mullings is a talented, driven, and high-achieving man. To be painfully honest, he strikes many people as a little odd.

This is not to say that he isn't handsome and charming by conventional standards - he is. Nor is it to say that his screenwriting, which is already winning prizes, isn't accessible and gripping - it is.

But Jay has a look in his eye; that of a man who knows who and what he wants to be and where and when he's going. He also isn't afraid to tell you what he thinks you should be doing (which in my case is writing this foreword).

People like this make you argue. Some times you agree with them. Sometimes you disagree. And sometimes they make you see things - and yourself - in a different light.

This book can be used to tell you about Jay, and the way he sees things. I'm not against that. I like and respect him. But there is another way to read - one that I think is better.

Reading this book helps you to know and to defend yourself. Listen carefully, and then argue with Jay on the many occasions when you resent him telling you things you feel you knew already, or asserting things that can't be true for reasons you have yet to formulate. He makes you defend yourself; he makes you remind yourself of what you know; he makes you decide the real reasons why you believe things.

And this, I believe, is what the book is really for.

Introduction

This book is a conversation. It is for you, but it is by me. These are the thoughts that have helped to steady me on my journey. This is the fuel that has kept me going. Throughout my sternest tests, these are the words that have toughened my resolve. This is the way I think and how I balance my scale.

The reason I have chosen this style and layout is simply to invite you to absorb the information quickly and even add your own comments either below, or on the last ten pages of this book if the impulse takes you. These have been intentionally left blank for you to fill with your own thoughtful words.

Mental strength is not as simple as having it or not. Even those who have had it can temporarily lose it. 'The Thought Book' is a guide to your true self. You remember, the strong, assured, charming, beautiful and intelligent you?

Without further ado, I present, 'The Thought Book'…

*W*e all start from somewhere.
There is no shame in being a novice
in pursuit of becoming a master.

*J*ust because it hasn't been done yet, doesn't mean you can't be the first…

$\mathscr{P}$erspective
is important in
all things…

JAY *Mullings*

Anyone who's ever blazed a trail has done so in the hopes of inspiring others.

12

*W*orrying about things just gives you more cause to worry. Break the cycle!

You have the power!
You can tell your feelings of doubt
to be quiet at any time.

14

*S*elf dialogue can be healthy.
If you can reconcile with yourself;
everyone else is a lot easier.

JAY *Mullings*

The mind is a powerful tool
when married to purpose.

*P*ut positive thoughts
into your mind and watch
your life change for the better.
The universe is watching…

Feelings of doubt I refuse
to harbour. I refuse to be broken,
I'll reinforce my armour.

*M*y desire to achieve burns hotter than lava. If no one believes in me; all I'll do is try harder…

The only barriers to success
that exist are the ones
you acknowledge.

$\mathcal{F}$ollow your instincts;
when right, they lead you to
the most beautiful experiences...

*R*eserve a special place
in your heart and mind for
keeping your dreams alive.

$\mathscr{P}$ractice is required to make anything look effortless; this is the worlds worst kept secret.

JAY *Mullings*

$\mathcal{B}$etter to live a life of dream chasing than to bury them prematurely.

THE *Thought* BOOK

$\mathcal{W}$hen in pursuit of your dreams,
be understanding of those who look
at you as crazy. Your journey
will prove otherwise…

25

*N*ot everyone can understand
the intensity that goes with
attempting to be extraordinary.

Anything that threatens your happiness should become your primary motivation in life.

JAY *Mullings*

*B*eing told you're not good enough can be a wakeup call or a dream killer. It's always up to you...

28

*L*et nothing stand in the way of what you truly want in life. If life pushes you, push back harder!

Sometimes you have to be a force of nature. Decide to be unstoppable in your pursuit of success.

THE *Thought* BOOK

$\mathscr{U}$se your difficulties
as motivation for making
your life easier.

Keep on moving in spite of
every obstacle thrown at you...
That is the true definition
of character.

*E*verything is about timing;
keep working on yourself and
your time will come.

My dreams
don't haunt me
they motivate me.

$\mathscr{I}$'m changing
the game one level
at a time.

35

JAY *Mullings*

I know who I am, but more importantly; I know who I will be in the future.

THE *Thought* BOOK

The problems of today make victory in the future more rewarding.

Stop, think, reflect.
Believe, move, progress…

*E*ven the smallest
progress is still a move
in the right direction.

*M*OMENTUM...
It helps us progress to the completion of our goals.

I'm just crawling
until I'm strong enough to walk
and fast enough to run.

When I plan,
I don't forecast failure,
no matter the climate.

*F*ortune favours the brave,
success rewards the clinical.
Take the chances you make;
be brave & clinical.

*E*verything happens for
a reason. If not, then you
have a reason to make
everything happen.

THE *Thought* BOOK

I have a wide grin on my face,
I know what's ahead has
no choice but to obey my fate;
greatness awaits!

JAY *Mullings*

*A*ppreciate that you
have everything you need
to get everything you want.

46

I will meditate
then levitate to
get the job done.

$\mathcal{W}$hen you're strong mentally,
it's like jumping off a cliff knowing that
you're about to grow wings and fly.

THE *Thought* BOOK

$\mathscr{A}$ postive example
is the best way to avoid
a negative outcome.

Striving leads to thriving;
never forget.

THE *Thought* BOOK

At times it's hard to accept compliments out of fear they're untrue. Allow yourself to believe.

Look at yourself in the mirror.
Repeat after me,
"I am good enough!".

THE *Thought* BOOK

You are strong,
assured, intelligent
and beautiful…

53

JAY *Mullings*

The foundation has been set now to build something worthwhile on top.

THE *Thought* BOOK

Smile; you're alive
and full of hope for what
the day might bring.

From here on in, things
can either go smoothly or terribly.
I'm prepared either way.

THE *Thought* BOOK

$\mathscr{A}$nything that can be done today, should be done today. Tomorrow is not a promise...

57

Today is an indicator of what
we can achieve. Today is not
for clichés; but we must believe.

Today we stand proud and tall.
Today we climb to the top,
no step is too small.

JAY *Mullings*

Even the most meticulous
plan means nothing
if the work isn't done.

You're best is the light
in the darkest tunnel
that illuminates the rest…

I'm veracious, I'm valid, I'm quirky.
If my aim is true, I'll hit the top shortly.

THE *Thought* BOOK

$\mathcal{I}$'m ready, I'm relaxed, I'm grown.
If my heart was a kingdom,
my mind would be the throne.

*P*ay your dues;
just leave a little change
for blazing your own trail.

*I*f people are jealous of you,
it means you're doing something right.
Don't ever stop doing it!

JAY *Mullings*

When they shout, "You will never be anything" just whisper, "You're all wrong" then back it up.

*S*uccess can happen
at the first or last attempt.
Endeavour to stay motivated.

JAY *Mullings*

*W*inning is such a fragile thing.
You can either celebrate it
too short or way too long.

Challenges bring out the best
or worst in us depending on what
really exists beyond the exterior.

*A*void envying others.
What's theirs is theirs; focus
on getting what you want.

70

Do not look at others as a guide for evaluating yourself; you risk losing everything good about you.

Do not fear failure.
The experience illuminates
the path to success…

*F*utility is character building.
It helps us learn to let go
of things we can't control.

The bad times make the good times even sweeter. Ride the waves and stay the course.

THE *Thought* BOOK

Ignore the voice that tells you to quit because the journey has gotten treacherous. The best things come to those who persist with belief.

75

JAY *Mullings*

Sometimes you have to
go through the worst before you
get to the best. Keep going!

76

A ship at sea has to ride
the waves as they ebb and flow
while remaining on course.
Be the captain of your ship…

JAY *Mullings*

*W*ork at your craft;
it is guaranteed to build
character and skill…

78

$\mathcal{G}$ROWTH... It means many different things at different times, yet it's always an essential part of life.

JAY *Mullings*

*P*ress forwards, when the opportunity to do so comes; go for it with confidence.

80

*I*t's okay to reward yourself
for how far you've come as long as
your focus remains on getting better.

*M*ake time to rejuvenate.
Even the most reliable machines
need time for maintenance.

THE *Thought* BOOK

Sleep to rest;
arise to live your dreams...

83

There are times when you need to put yourself 1st, 2nd & 3rd. Only selfish people won't understand this.

THE *Thought* BOOK

I'm not someone that
needs the approval of others
to be happy.

JAY *Mullings*

Communication
is a two way process,
you and I know that.

Length of time having known someone does not guarantee longevity of friendship.

JAY *Mullings*

So called friends with
your interests at heart. Behind
your back, they're throwing the
sharpest darts.

88

THE *Thought* BOOK

*I*t kills them inside
to see you do well. Instead of
congratulating you, they make
up lies to tell...

JAY *Mullings*

*I*n a true friendship,
a victory for one
is a victory for all.

THE *Thought* BOOK

$\mathscr{A}$nyone can spread rumours.
A superior being agrees both not
to create or acknowledge them.

JAY *Mullings*

If I show you kindness
and you show disrespect,
I'll just laugh at your stupidity.

I'm not drawn to indifference.
I go where I'm wanted.

JAY *Mullings*

The 'I' in win
sometimes gets in the way
of forming a great team.

$\mathcal{I}$f you have more enemies than friends, you either inspire envy or hate.

*S*ome people derive energy
from destroying yours.
Take that away from them and
watch them struggle to survive.

My circle is like a forcefield.
Absolutely no entry
for undersirables…

JAY *Mullings*

People will see what they
want to see; all you can do
is try to brighten their
field of vision.

*C*onnection requires
common objectives.
The frequency is unimportant if
the wavelength matches.

Hardship can make
or break a relationship.

THE *Thought* BOOK

A little tough love
goes a long way.
Use it responsibly…

JAY *Mullings*

*N*ever look down on
others for being brave
enough to ask for help.

102

Being kind beats
being cool in my eyes.

JAY *Mullings*

$\mathcal{T}$ouch peoples lives positively whenever you can. Even the smallest acts of kindness go a long way.

104

*S*ee your worth when you stare into a mirror. Show you friends their own when they are blind to it.

$\mathcal{B}$e the friend that is fair
in every regard and the same
shall be returned to you.

THE *Thought* BOOK

*I*f your friends don't push
you to be your best,
you need new ones.

JAY *Mullings*

*F*riends make life bearable.
They'll either help you off the ground
or encourage you to get up.

108

I'm quirky!
I try to keep people who
can accept that around.

*I*t is never weak to let the people around you know they melt your heart. Strength can be derived from a reason to live.

*N*ever forget to acknowledge
the people who supported you
on your way up.

Friends that are invested or
interested in your growth
are the best kind.

The people that add value to your life are truly invaluable. Always account for appreciating them.

JAY *Mullings*

*O*ur choices
determine whether
we rise or fall…

114

Desire is a double edged sword,
handle it with care.

JAY *Mullings*

$\mathscr{S}$tamina is a prerequisite
when you want to be successful.

116

THE *Thought* BOOK

*I*t should never feel wrong to
do something right,
nor should it feel right to
do something wrong.

JAY *Mullings*

*I*f it's not what you say but
how you say it,
then it's not what you do but
how you do it.

118

*I*f you wish to know how strong you are, measure by how restrained you are with it.

JAY *Mullings*

A true hero does heroic deeds without the need for praise. Recognition is to be earned, not expected.

Your goal should be
to take a rough life easy. Not
to make an easy life rough.

JAY *Mullings*

Don't be about stereotypes
and the obvious, be more.

THE *Thought* BOOK

There are those whose dream
it is to oppress. For each of those,
there is one with the wish to progress.

JAY *Mullings*

*N*o excuse for moral bankruptcy.
We need to be as shrewd
as the clergy.

124

THE *Thought* BOOK

$\mathcal{L}$apses in judgement are an inevitable part of life. Accept their lessons to lessen the impact.

You should take in
the wisdom of your elders
like a vacuum does dust.

There is a reason people mellow
with time. Constant battling
wears on the soul...

JAY *Mullings*

$\mathscr{F}$alse humility is like counterfeit money. You can't fool everyone with it.

128

I am grateful as each day goes by;
I become more patient and wise
than the one before.

JAY *Mullings*

Outer beauty means nothing
if it hides a rotten core…

*O*ur sacrifices don't have to be the same for them to be meaningful.

JAY *Mullings*

$\mathcal{C}$almness and stillness
aren't always the same thing.
Know which to choose…

Complacency moves
with stealth, sometimes we miss it
creeping up on us.

JAY *Mullings*

True consciousness
cannot be faked; it's simply
incontrovertible.

134

*J*ust because something is done differently than how you would do it, doesn't give you permission to be disrespectful.

The best thing for you...
Is to be really good at
being you.

There can only be one you.
Why waste time trying
to be anyone else?

JAY *Mullings*

*N*o one on this earth is perfect.
Don't be fooled into thinking you
need to be…

138

THE *Thought* BOOK

I don't yearn for everyone to understand me. In fact, I think I'm suited to being misunderstood.

I will never stop believing in myself; so it's ok if you don't believe in me.

There is nothing more valuable
than a clear mind.

*M*editation is
the gateway to relaxation.
Adequate preparation is the key.

Your health is very important.
Avoid practices which
jeopardise that.

JAY *Mullings*

$\mathscr{I}$'m a logical person.
I don't waste energy trying to see
logic where there is none.

You and I can never be the same.
We should always agree on that.

I do things my way
and that way is always
alright with me.

$\mathcal{R}$eturn to the basics of life,
that's the best way to handle the
more complex things it asks of you.

JAY *Mullings*

The joy of life is in living
up to your potential
as a complete being.

Your life can be fulfilling;
all you need to be is willing.

JAY *Mullings*

Self confidence
attracts confidence in you
from others.

Remain stable, there is no need to overreact!

JAY *Mullings*

$\mathcal{T}$urning the other cheek is meek. Turning your back is naïve. Walking away is smart!

152

THE *Thought* BOOK

I fight with my inner demons
and sometimes we all have
a drink together after…

*M*y life is a sitcom. So please,
keep your drama away from me
at all times!

 I'm saying no to drama
by remaining calmer. You reap
what you sow; I believe they
call it karma.

Your essence is like the sea.
Do you prefer serene
or tumultuous waters?

*P*ain gives you a long memory; happiness gives you a longer life. Choose wisely…

Wishful Thinking

Jay Mullings

Sometimes I zone out and stay there
I let my thoughts integrate with the atmosphere
Not everything I say is always right, let us be clear

However, it comes from a good place, look, right here
A confused heart with a thoughtful mind,
harmony is so rare

With great thoughts comes the undeniable onus to share
I try not to be selfish, so I openly declare
Deliberately spreading the word to everyone everywhere

Harsh truths that wake you from your living nightmare
Alerting you to your potential,
finally breathing the belief in the air

Rationale reprogrammed, relaxing the impulse to swear
There is no longer frustration;
it has been replaced with your flair.

Acknowledgement

Thank you; such a simple thing to say, yet there are times it cannot truly capture someone's immense feelings of appreciation. My friends, (You know yourselves) naming you all would require longer paper and a much smaller font. You are all profoundly loved. To my doubters, you have looked down on me and often tried to discourage me from pursuing my passion. I thank you sincerely; you helped mould a more resilient spirit. To my family (Insert your name here), I thank you enormously; I know there are times when I've appeared withdrawn or possessed by my ideas. Thank you greatly for not having me committed (smile). Last but not at all least, you, the reader, your support is overwhelmingly humbling. You help keep my fire alive.

Thank you all for playing a part in my journey.

@writtenmirror
#thethoughtbook

THE *Thought* BOOK

@writtenmirror
#thethoughtbook

JAY *Mullings*

@writtenmirror
#thethoughtbook

THE *Thought* BOOK

@writtenmirror
#thethoughtbook

163

@writtenmirror
#thethoughtbook

THE *Thought* BOOK

@writtenmirror
#thethoughtbook

165

JAY *Mullings*

@writtenmirror
#thethoughtbook

THE *Thought* BOOK

@writtenmirror
#thethoughtbook